# The Bright Son

**Written by Maurice Williams**
**Illustration by Julián Galván**

Butterscotch Memoirs

ISBN 978-0-9885227-4-9

**Printed in the United States of America**

Design: Julián Galván  |  www.juliangalvan.com.ar

On a warm and relaxing summer afternoon, Howard Jackson sat in his study reading the day's newspaper. The warm rays of the sun shone through a nearby open window. His son, Thomas, age 10, made the most of the day as he rode his bicycle around the neighborhood. Wearing a bright yellow helmet and kneepads, Thomas took advantage of the weather and zipped through the neighboring fields like a busy honeybee.

As Howard read his newspaper, the telephone rang. The caller announced herself as Ms. Morrow, Thomas' schoolteacher.

"Mr. Jackson, I'm so sorry to bother you," she said.

"Oh, it's not a bother, Ms. Morrow," Howard replied.

"The last time we spoke, you asked me to call you if I had any concerns about Thomas. Well, I have been noticing something in class. Thomas has not been volunteering like he normally does. It appears that Thomas is intentionally blending in to the rest of the class instead of leading from the front. He rarely raises his hand to answer questions anymore and he did not turn in his last homework assignment on time" she said.

Howard listened for several minutes while watching Thomas ride his bike. After the discussion, Howard thanked Ms. Morrow for keeping him updated.

"Son, come and see me for a minute," Howard called out to Thomas.

"Yes, Dad," Thomas replied, out of breath from all of the hard riding. Thomas made his way into the house, removing his bicycle helmet.

"Come and have a seat, Son," Howard said.

"Yes, sir," Thomas replied.

"Is there anything that we need to talk about, Son? And as always, think before you respond," Howard said.

Thomas paused. He knew his father well and was aware that his father appeared to magically know about everything he did. He decided to tell the truth.

"Well, Dad, I have been kind of distracted lately," Thomas said.

With a raised brow, Howard said, "Funny, I heard the exact same thing from your teacher, Ms. Morrow."

Thomas lowered his head in shame. He knew he should have come to his father and been honest about what was going on.

"Son, lift your head and come and stand in the middle of the floor," Howard instructed. The concerned father gently slid the living room coffee table to the side to make room for his son to stand before him, and took a comfortable seat on the couch in front of Thomas, as he stood motionless.
Howard sat with his hand on his cheek, waiting patiently for Thomas to begin. "The stage is yours, Son," he said, sighing.

Thomas had been on this stage before. "Well, Dad," he said.

His father cut him off, slowly pointed his finger, and said, "Think, breathe, then allow the truth to flow."

Thomas was nervous as he stood
at attention in front of his Father.
"I know, Dad," he whispered.

"Are you ready to proceed, Son?"
Howard asked his only child.
"Yes, sir," Thomas responded.

"Dad, I haven't been raising my hand in class that much, well, not as much as I used to," he said.

"I'm listening," his father replied.

"Ms. Morrow always calls on me to answer questions, but that's just not cool, Dad. My friends laugh at me and call me corny," Thomas painfully said.

"How does that make you feel, Son?" Howard asked.

"I don't like it, Dad," Thomas replied. "Why do I have to be different? Why do I have to be the smart one?" Thomas' eyes lowered and he fidgeted with his hands.

Howard paused and shook his head slowly before responding. "Son, look at me." Thomas raised his eyes to look at his father. "What have I always told you about a quality education?"

"I know, Dad, but…"

Howard cut Thomas off mid sentence. "No, not 'I know, Dad.' What exactly have we discussed about the three keys to education?"

"Education is the key to unlocking every door. Education is the key difference between success and failure," Thomas said.

"And finally?" Howard asked.

"Yes, sir. The final key is that he who reads, leads," Thomas said.

18

Howard nodded in approval as his only child effortlessly recited the motto he has instilled in him since he was old enough to read.

"Now, Son, help me understand how turning your back on your education fits in with anything that you just recited," Howard asked.

Thomas did not respond.

"I can't hear you, Son," Howard uttered. "Explain to me why you want to be someone else, why you want to be a follower. Help me understand why a brilliant young man wants to hide his gifts so that his so-called friends will like him."

In a softened voice, Thomas said, "I just want to have friends. I want them to like me." His eyes began to water.

Howard could see the pain and conflict Thomas was experiencing. He told his son to sit next to him on the couch. "Thomas, you are a brilliant young man. You're filled with emotions right now and you're trying to figure out where you fit in. I know this because I went through the exact same thing."

"You did?" Thomas asked.

"I absolutely did. When I was your age, I was placed in gifted and talented education classes because I scored higher than my classmates on tests. I was separated from my friends. I didn't like it at the time, but it paid off in the end," Howard said.

"Do you understand what I am saying, Son? Do you understand why you need to allow your bright light to shine?"

"Yes, Dad. You always tell me to be a leader and not follow the crowd. I guess it's starting to make sense to me now," Thomas said.

The young man dried his eyes and hugged his father. "I love you, Dad, and I promise to talk to you about anything that's bothering me in the future."

"I love you too, Son, and know that I'll always be there for you," Howard said.

After their embrace, Thomas grabbed his helmet and bicycle and headed back out into the sunny afternoon, with a brighter perspective on life and the knowledge of the importance of embracing his gifts and blazing a glowing trail of educational excellence.

# THE END

# From the author

**Maurice Williams** enjoys the extraordinary voyage associated with creative writing and original storytelling.

As a fan of a variety of genres, his writings include a host of different topics and subject matter.

Maurice holds a B.S. degree in Administration of Justice from Texas Southern University. He is also a proud Veteran of the United States Army.

www.ingramcontent.com/pod-product-compliance
Lightning Source LLC
LaVergne TN
LVHW072110070426
835509LV00002B/104